KERRY ANN ROUSE

Breast Reduction Made Simple:

Preparation, Healing, and Beyond

First published by Platypus Publishing 2025

Copyright © 2025 by Kerry Ann Rouse

All rights reserved. No part of this publication may be reproduced, stored or transmitted in any form or by any means, electronic, mechanical, photocopying, recording, scanning, or otherwise without written permission from the publisher. It is illegal to copy this book, post it to a website, or distribute it by any other means without permission.

Kerry Ann Rouse has no responsibility for the persistence or accuracy of URLs for external or third-party Internet Websites referred to in this publication and does not guarantee that any content on such Websites is, or will remain, accurate or appropriate.

Designations used by companies to distinguish their products are often claimed as trademarks. All brand names and product names used in this book and on its cover are trade names, service marks, trademarks and registered trademarks of their respective owners. The publishers and the book are not associated with any product or vendor mentioned in this book. None of the companies referenced within the book have endorsed the book.

First edition

Advisor: Dr. Jason D. Johnson - double board certified plastic surgeon
Cover art by Ryan Moreno on Unsplash

This book was professionally typeset on Reedsy.
Find out more at reedsy.com

To Mike, the absolute love of my life.

Contents

Acknowledgments   iii
Introduction   1

I   Part One

1   I AM LIKE YOU   7
2   FINDING A SURGEON   12
3   THE CONSULTATION   19
4   SUBSTANCES   23
5   FINANCIAL COST   28
6   TIME OFF WORK/SCHOOL   32
7   YOUR SUPPORT SYSTEM   36
8   GATHER YOUR SUPPLIES   39
9   BEFORE PHOTOS   44
10   FOLLOWING INSTRUCTIONS   47
11   PREPARING YOURSELF   50

II   Part Two

12   THE DAY OF SURGERY   59
13   THE FIRST WEEK   66
14   THE SECOND WEEK   74
15   WEEKS 3-6   81
16   THE MAGIC LINE   83

17	ACCEPTANCE	94
18	BODY DYSMORPHIA	96
19	ACTUAL HARM	98
20	THE RESULTS	101

| 21 | Conclusion | 104 |
| *About the Author* | | 106 |

Acknowledgments

I give special thanks to Dr. Jason D. Johnson of Phx Plastic Surgery in Peoria, Arizona. I am grateful for the guidance and information provided for this book, and for the stellar medical care I received.

Introduction

A woman without breasts is like a bed without pillows.
-Anatole France

I have wanted to have a breast reduction for over two decades. My breasts have been too large and droopy for a long time, and I've often fantasized about having them "fixed". When the time finally came to have the procedure, I started to ponder the importance of breasts. I never had children, so why do I need them? What is it about breasts that makes them so important to me?

Breasts are an important part of a woman's identity and sexual life. Having breasts that are too big and heavy can create image anxieties. It makes us feel ugly and can cause pain and stress on the body. When we experience these anxieties related to our breasts, it can affect our comfort level with intimacy. Some experts believe that breast stimulation activates neurological pathways that are similar to mother-infant bonding which contribute to a deep emotional connection between partners. But it's more than that. Breasts make us *feel* like women.

Breast reduction surgery was essential to me. I wanted to alleviate the physical discomfort of having too large breasts such as back, neck, and shoulder pain. I wanted to improve my body image and look more proportional. I wanted to improve my confidence, wear a wider variety of clothing, and improve my posture. I also wanted to be able to perform various forms of exercise with no limitations imposed on me by my breasts.

If you are reading this, you are in the same boat. If you've decided breast reduction surgery is your solution, then this book is for you.

Why write this book?

I want to help you. I've experienced what it was like to undergo a breast reduction and relied on sage advice to get me through it. I'm so grateful to everyone who helped me.

I speak to many women, and I know the burning questions we all have. I know the anxiety before, during and after the surgery. I'll be here for you when the days are rough, like a supportive friend who understands. I want to give you ideas that had not occurred to you before, and even offer some advice that can save your life.

Are you a medical expert?

I am not a medical professional of any kind, and this book is not a replacement for the advice of your own doctor. Your doctor knows your entire medical history, and my doctor knows mine. You and I could be very different in age, health, and pain tolerance. That is why I have spoken to so many women and have consulted with a plastic surgeon to write this book.

I will be joined by various women's voices who have had the procedure and have healed. My advice is offered in friendship, and if it can help you

INTRODUCTION

undergo a breast reduction procedure easier and with more comfort, than I have done my job.

I

Part One

The decision to embrace a life-changing transformation is a powerful act of self-love and courage. It is the moment when you choose growth over fear, strength over doubt, and possibility over limitation. Each step forward is a declaration that you deserve a life filled with confidence and joy. Transformation is about reclaiming your sense of self, honoring your needs, and stepping into a future where you feel free and whole.

1

I AM LIKE YOU

Who has more fun? Blondes or brunettes?
The girls with the bigger boobs!
-Unknown

We are probably a bit similar when it comes to breasts. Many of us share a similar story.

I exploded into puberty at a very young age, and I was suddenly taller than all of my classmates. My breasts grew so fast that I ended up a C cup by the time I was in the 6th grade. The other girls in my girl scout troop called me "Stuffy" because they started a rumor that I stuffed my bra. The name transferred over to my grade school, and all the girls made fun of me daily. (I put a stop to that when I flashed them in the school bathroom!) My mother explained to me that they were just jealous, but I know now that wasn't true. The other kids just weren't ready to see C-cups in the sixth grade.

By the time I was in high school, I was a D-cup. I started to get a lot of attention from boys, and I relished it. Almost every boy I dated told me that one of the best things about me was my "sweet rack". I was too young and naïve to understand this was not necessarily a good thing to put my self-worth in what boys thought of me. But for me, after being teased for so long, it felt like suddenly everything about me was okay! I directly linked my self-esteem to how the world was responding to my looks.

Grade school = boobs are bad. Adulthood = boobs are great!

> *I know my breasts have opened doors for me, let's be real.*
> *-Sophia Vergara*

> *Scientists now believe that the primary biological function of breasts is to make males stupid.*
> *-Dave Barry*

I pleasantly discovered how much men love breasts, so I leaned into it. I wore sexy push up bras, and I enjoyed showing off my womanly figure. For many years, my breasts were extremely important to my identity. I was the sexy, busty, voluptuous diva!

Over the years, I gained and lost a lot of weight. I have weighed over 300 pounds more than once in my life, and have lost the weight more than once. This did not benefit the boobies. Although I never had children, by the time I was in my 40s, my breasts were stretched out, droopy, and bigger than ever. My nipples looked like big pink pepperonis.

I had to buy plus sized bras that felt like torture devices with wide ugly straps. My great comfort at the end of the day was taking off my bra and getting into my pajamas. When I sat on the couch, my boobs were literally laying in my lap. When my pups came up onto my lap, they walked all over my nipples.

I'm sure you can relate to the following symptoms:

I had pain in my shoulders and back. Carrying pounds of extra weight on your chest takes its toll on your back and can create recurring pain. I also felt pain and numbness from bra straps digging into my shoulders. I had permanent indentations there.

I got sores under my breasts when the weather was hot because of the under boob sweating. I tried to treat the sores with antibiotic cream. I tried to prevent the sores with baby powder, but still they came back. I didn't always get sores, but when I did, they were a major irritant.

I didn't look good in any clothes. I had to buy bigger clothes to accommodate my chest, and everything looked the same. Everything tugged tightly against my breasts, no matter the cut or style. (I have learned that clothes designers make clothes for B-cups.)

All my choices in tops had to include thick straps or sleeves to hide my wide bra straps. One of my major problems is that big girl bras are expensive! I have paid as much as $80-$100 for a reliable supportive bra. These bras are generally not made in the racerback style, so I had to forget about wearing most tank tops. I could only dream of wearing a strapless dress or tops with spaghetti straps.

Sadie resting in one of my bra cups

I had to scoop up my boobs and make sure the nipples were pointing forward every time I put on a bra. No matter how much I hiked them up, they slipped downward and pointed toward the floor throughout the day. I had to keep reaching into my bra throughout the day to readjust.

My breasts spilled out of the top of my bra. If I bent over to pick something up or to clean, my cleavage came spilling out. I took up a yoga practice a few years ago, and during that time I just got used to my breasts falling into my face when I was doing Downward Dog.

This is no way for a woman to live! I finally decided to do something very important to me: I decided to have Breast Reduction surgery.

What next?

I did my research, scheduled a consultation, and chose a fantastic surgeon to do my surgery. And yes, I'm going to tell you all about it!

After I scheduled my surgery, I immediately went on the hunt for what I needed. I did a lot of research and found ways to make the experience as smooth and comfortable as possible. I bought some supplies that proved to be extremely valuable for my comfort while recovering.

I learned a great deal about what to wear, how to care for my wounds, how to manage the pain, how to shower, what I could and couldn't do, what bras to wear, and more. I will share my sage advice regarding hygiene, "zingers", stretching and exercise, and I'll address going back to work. I'll also address the emotional aspects of the experience, from excitement to anxiety and more.

Out of all the plastic surgery procedures that are done, the patients who have had breast reductions are statistically the happiest with their outcomes. I experienced great relief and even joy after mine.

The following chapters will outline everything I learned and want to share, in chronological order. I'll start from finding a great surgeon, to the days when I got back on my feet.

2

FINDING A SURGEON

> She got her looks from her father. He's a plastic surgeon.
> -Groucho Marx

One of the best ways I set myself up for success was by finding an excellent surgeon. Plastic surgery is not just a medical procedure, it's also an art form, and it requires years and years of education and training. Breast reductions are a bit more complex than your average breast augmentation or liposuction procedure.

Unfortunately, the government does not regulate cosmetic procedures. Any type of doctor, and I do mean ANY type, can perform cosmetic procedures. He could be an OB/GYN, a family doctor, a dermatologist, nurse practitioner, or even a dentist. If he decides he wants to make more money doing breast work, he may simply watch a YouTube video or attend a single conference and then begin to do surgical procedures. I knew it was essential to my health and well-being to avoid these shady characters. The only type of doctor I felt safe with was a plastic surgeon.

I'll begin by explaining the educational standards for a well-trained and highly skilled plastic surgeon.

Undergraduate Degree – The first step is to go to college and get a bachelor's degree in majors such as biology, chemistry, or a pre-med track. This takes four years to complete. The student must then sit for the MCAT exam for entry into medical school.

Medical School – The second step is to obtain a medical degree which as either an MD or DO. This takes at least four years to complete.

Licensure – For the third step, the doctor will then be evaluated by a licensing board. The board will conduct a thorough background investigation to include educational history, and will research thoroughly to uncover any malpractice claims or criminal activity. This step takes approximately 2-4 months.

At this point, the surgeon can take one of two paths.

1. Residency in plastic surgery – 6 years. This training delves deeply into primarily reconstructive procedures (repairing injuries, post mastectomy reconstruction or congenital deformities, to name a few) and includes cosmetic procedures.
2. General Surgery Residency for 5 years, and a plastic surgery fellowship for 2-3 years. This path delves deeply into surgery of many types, with intense training in reconstructive and cosmetic procedures. This path entails 7-8+ years of total surgical experience.

During the years of residency and fellowship, the surgeon will evaluate patients, assist in surgery, attend clinics, practice in various surgical labs, and will take on progressively more difficult cases and more responsibility. This comprehensive background ensures they are well-equipped to handle both complex cases and cosmetic procedures.

Board Certification – The next step is becoming board certified with the American Board of Plastic Surgery. The surgeon must pass a comprehensive oral and written examination, covering all aspects of plastic surgery. Board certification also requires the surgeon to continue ongoing medical education to stay up to date with the most current practices.

You can check the status of the doctor's credentials by going to ABMS | American Board of Medical Specialties. This will tell you if the surgeon has any complaints that were reported to the board.

Another indication that your plastic surgeon is highly skilled is that he has a voluntary membership in a professional organization such as The American Society of Plastic Surgeons. This shows the doctor is committed to continually learning, adheres to a code of ethics, and has completed all the necessary training.

One of the most important considerations is this: Does the surgeon have hospital privileges? If he has privileges in an accredited hospital, this means the surgeon meets the hospital's rigorous standards for patient care. It also means that if something happens unexpectedly that requires hospitalization (some tissue becomes dead, a serious infection occurs, or any other possible emergency) then your surgeon will be able to come to the hospital and treat you. Unfortunately, if a doctor does not have hospital privileges and you have a serious complication, he will just send you to the emergency room and another doctor who's never met you will be treating you. Also, the additional surgeon who does the follow-up care would not be covered in your initial surgical cost.

Q: I see all kinds of cosmetic surgeons advertising. What if he's a cosmetic surgeon?

Cosmetic surgeons, on the other hand, specialize exclusively in cosmetic procedures. Cosmetic surgeons may complete a general surgical residency and then complete a one to two-year fellowship in cosmetic surgery. This means their training is narrowly focused on only aesthetic procedures, and they generally lack the broader surgical experience of a plastic surgeon.

Another important consideration is that the American Board of Cosmetic Surgery is not recognized by the government as a valid medical board. (It is not recognized by the American Board of Medical Specialties.)

When cosmetic surgeons complete their training, they have completed approximately 600+ surgeries, as opposed to a plastic surgeon who has completed several thousand.

Another, and potentially more dangerous type of "cosmetic surgeon", might not even be a surgeon at all. Many "cosmetic surgeons" could be nurse practitioners, anesthesiologists, dentists, GI's, physician assistants, or even naturopaths who watched YouTube videos, read an article, or even took a one day course with no hands-on experience. You could be the first patient they've ever performed surgery on with no formal training or oversight.

Do not be fooled by tricky wording on web sites such as "studied at the

Mayo Clinic" (this could mean just one workshop was completed), and names such as "Dr. Dave" or "superfun lipo". They may advertise that they are board certified without listing in what specialty. They may also be vague about who would be doing your procedure, the credentials and training, and may state that they could perform invasive surgery in a makeshift exam room in their office.

Also don't be fooled by social media following or random "awards". Both of these things can be simply bought.

If a doctor says that he doesn't **need** hospital privileges for whatever reason, this is a huge red flag! Again, you want to ensure that he meets the rigorous standards and if any complications arise that require further treatment at a hospital, your surgeon will be able to treat you.

Q: This is all a little confusing. Tell me what to look for when I am searching for a surgeon. What will I see on their website?

To boil it down, you want a surgeon who is board certified by the American Board of Plastic Surgery, and who has hospital privileges. The web site should clearly state where they graduated and what they specialized in.

Q: Should I find an older doctor with more experience?

Even younger plastic surgeons start their careers having already completed six to ten years of focused surgical training. They've worked approximately 25,000-35,000 hours under direct supervision of senior surgeons. Even surgeons who are just starting out still have great expertise.

FINDING A SURGEON

Q: How did you find your surgeon?

There are many ways to find a great surgeon because they advertise. I literally used google and found the nearest plastic surgeon. I live in a tiny little mountain town in Arizona, so I wanted someone within a reasonable driving distance. Dr. Jason D. Johnson's web site clearly displayed his double board certification and education, and displayed some promising before and after pictures, so I made an appointment for a consultation.

At the consultation, I immediately felt comfortable with him and his office staff. I didn't even have to get out my list of questions. In the consultation, he examined me and explained his plan for my surgery thoroughly. He advised me of the risks, advised me on how I can reduce my risks, and briefly walked me through the healing process. He offered me information that I didn't even know I needed to know. I mulled it over and decided I didn't need to see a second surgeon for a consultation. For me, I knew I would be in good hands with Dr. Johnson and his office staff.

I do recommend that if you have a consultation with a surgeon and you're just not sure if you like the procedure as he described it, or you are left with too many unanswered questions, then schedule a second consultation with another surgeon. In fact, many women go to more than one doctor's office for a consultation before choosing a surgeon.

Q: Did you ever think about going to Mexico? Surgery is much cheaper there!

Oh yes, I definitely thought about it since I live very near the border. Procedures in Mexico are cheaper which can be tempting. Many clinics in popular medical tourism destinations, such as Tijuana and Guadalajara, cater to international patients and boast highly trained surgeons, some of whom have received education and certifications in the US or Europe.

But there are risks involved with traveling to Mexico for plastic surgery. One primary concern is the variation in quality and safety standards among clinics. While many facilities are reputable, others may lack proper accreditation, increasing the risk of complications or subpar outcomes. Language barriers and differences in post-operative care protocols can also make communication and follow-up treatment challenging.

And you also have to ask yourself: What if something goes wrong and complications arise after returning home? You'll just end up being sent to the emergency room. Finding a surgeon willing to address the issues from an out-of-country procedure can be difficult and expensive.

My surgeon stated that he sees botched surgeries for patients who went to Mexico at least once a week. These patients do not want to go back to Mexico for follow-up care because their experience was so negative.

Now that you know the rigorous education and training required for a plastic surgeon, I hope you will follow my advice and find a great board certified plastic surgeon with hospital privileges.

3

THE CONSULTATION

My husband said "show me your boobs" and I had to pull up my skirt...
so it was time to get them done.
-Dolly Parton

Before I went to the consultation, I thought long and hard about what I really wanted. I was sick to death of having such large breasts that I wanted to have what I would describe as "humble" breasts. I looked at a lot of before and after pictures and found several that looked like me before, so I focused on their results when setting my expectations.

Prior to the consultation, the office sent me a lot of paperwork to fill out, specifically my medical history and a list of prescriptions that I take. I arrived at the office and signed in. I was then taken to an exam room, and they gave me a front opening paper top to change into.

The surgeon and his assistant joined me and we discussed my goals. I explained to Dr. Johnson that I did not want them to bounce and sway when I walk. I was hoping to go from DDD/F to a C-cup with very little jiggle. The doctor explained that he would do his best to give me the results I wanted, but he warned me that I would have to leave the exact sizing up to him.

One of the most important considerations when performing breast reduction surgery is to keep the nipples alive. During surgery, the nipples are placed higher on the breasts, and there are very important arteries that run through the breasts to the nipples. If there are any problems with blood flow, one or both of the nipples could die and fall off. The reason this matters to you is that your surgeon has to decide how much tissue he can remove, and a lot of it depends on blood flow.

Dr. Johnson was clear and patient when discussing this in detail, and I grew to trust his judgment in the operating room. I decided that I would rather be a little bigger than I wanted than lose a nipple.

Another thing he explained thoroughly is that I would have visible scars. Having a breast reduction is trading in your big, saggy breasts for smaller, perkier breasts with scars. These scars do fade over time but will never entirely go away. The incisions are made around the nipple, straight downward from the breasts and then under the

Q: What information will the surgeon ask me?

The office will ask you a series of questions, either by filling out a form or verbally. They will ask you the standard questions such as your medical history, any past surgeries, any allergies, and so on. Come prepared with a list of any prescriptions and supplements that you take.

It's crucially important that you are completely honest. I know, I know... if you drink more than a few drinks a week, it's hard to be honest. If you dabble a bit with drugs, you might feel ashamed or might worry that the doctor won't take your case. I understand all of these worries. But take it from me, woman to woman, a smooth recovery depends on your honesty.

Q: I really don't want to reveal all that. What happens if I hold something back?

The short answer is that holding back important information such as substance or alcohol use could cause serious complications with your surgery. I do intend to scare you when I say that these secrets could even lead to death.

You should expect to be examined, photographed, and then to have a thorough conversation about your goals. Be as specific as you can about what you want and listen to the surgeon's recommendations. He doesn't have to be Mr. Charming, as long as he is patient and thorough. You should walk out of his office feeling like you have all the information you need to make a decision.

4

SUBSTANCES

An over-indulgence of anything, even something as pure as water, can intoxicate.
-Criss Jami

This is an important time in your life. Being off work is great, but this is no time to party. Your entire focus needs to be recovery and healing. Drugs and alcohol don't play a positive role in healing.

Alcohol

Most surgeons recommend abstaining from alcohol for at least three weeks prior to surgery. After surgery, alcohol is strictly prohibited while taking the narcotic pain medication. I can't say this strongly enough: If you drink alcohol, do not drink while taking your pain medication. This could cause serious problems with excessive bleeding, slowing of your heart rate, or even death. Your life is worth so much more.

If you feel you cannot stop drinking alcohol for this surgery, there are various options to help you stop, at least for the surgery.

- "The Alcohol Experiment" by Annie Grace is a great book that I've read and highly recommend. Many of us just need a bit of a nudge to make some changes.
- Find an in-person AA meeting. - You are not alone. There are AA meetings all over the world! You can easily find one near you by searching online. When you feel ashamed, walking into an AA meeting can be really scary for the first time. But all of the people in that room will accept you, not judge you, and will offer kindness and support. Sometimes that's all a person needs to begin to get a handle on the problem.
- Find online AA meetings – if there are no meetings close to you, or you want to just give them a try with little contact with others, attend an online meeting. Online meetings are going on right now, this very minute. No matter what time it is where you are, you can find an online meeting. Even if it's 4:00 in the morning.
- SMART recovery does not involve any type of religious or spiritual components. The SMART recovery system is to build and maintain motivation, cope with urges and cravings, manage thoughts, and live a balanced life. SMART recovery meetings can be found at https://meetings.smartrecovery.org. They also have meetings online.

Marijuana

When it comes to Marijuana, this is legal in most states and many people partake. My doctor's instructions were to stop using marijuana in any form for at least four weeks prior to surgery. Marijuana use can increase the amount of anesthesia needed, interfere with breathing, and slow healing. My surgeon advised that marijuana use could be resumed approximately a month after surgery.

Nicotene

If you are currently a smoker or a vaper, this one may be difficult for you. But you must stop smoking at least four to eight weeks before surgery. Smoking can increase your chances of some pretty serious complications:

- Smoking can damage the cilia in your lungs, creating more mucus and narrowing your airways. This could increase your risk of pneumonia or a collapsed lung.
- Smoking increases your heart rate and blood pressure and can reduce the amount of oxygen in your blood. This could result in you having a heart attack during or after surgery.
- Smoking could cause blood clots in your legs which can travel to your lungs and cause damage.
- Smokers are more likely to have complications related to anesthesia.
- Smoking causes a higher risk of infections of the chest and surgical wounds.

To put it plainly, smoking before surgery comes with a heightened risk of complications such as lung problems, heart problems, slower wound healing, and even coma or death. Even if you withhold from your surgeon that you smoke or vape, it will be discovered in your pre-surgical lab work.

Angie reminded me
  ...I had blood drawn two weeks before surgery and one item they screened for was nicotine.

But Cierra asked others how to quit:

I have to do labs so they can test my levels...and if I'm good to go, they'll schedule me but I'm STRUGGLING to quit vaping.

Jessica gave some great advice when she stated:

Swap the vaping liquid to 0% nicotine for now...That's what I did and ended up ditching the vape naturally...my surgeon was happy for me to vape on 0% nicotine.

Jessica also advised to buy a breathing necklace that can be purchased on Amazon. It's a small tube-like pendant that is designed to help you manage your breathing. I looked at the reviews on Amazon, and these do seem to help with quitting smoking.

Terra's review stated the following:

I ordered this hoping it would help me cut down on vaping, and I can already tell it's going to make a difference. I love that it's a necklace so it's always on hand when I feel the urge to reach for my vape pen. It won't help with nicotine cravings, but it's great to have something that mimics the hand-to-mouth motion without the vape clouds...I'm excited to see how much closer it brings me to quitting vaping for good.

Illegal drugs

Sometimes, you can only find Heaven by slowly backing away from Hell.
-Carrie Fisher

You probably know what I'm going to say here. Street drugs are illegal for a reason. They are unsafe for anyone at any time. If you take these drugs before surgery or during your healing process, you could end up with a variety of complications including excessive bleeding, heart problems, infections, an inability to heal, coma or death.

If you feel you cannot stop taking drugs for your surgery, please utilize your support system, and consider using outside resources for help.

- 988 – This is a crisis line that provides support and resources for various issues such as mental health problems, and drug or alcohol addiction.
- https://www.usa.gov/health – You can go to this website to find emergency hotlines, counseling, and treatment options for help with drug and alcohol addiction.
- https://dea.gov/recovery-resources – You can also use this website to find resources for a mental health condition or a substance use disorder.

5

FINANCIAL COST

> Money is better than poverty, if only for financial reasons.
> -Woody Allen

In the US, many women can have breast reduction surgery paid for by insurance. If your breasts are quite large, at least an F cup or over, insurance may cover yours. But if insurance does cover it, THEY determine your final size, not you. They use what's called the Schnurr Scale which uses a body surface area (BSA) to determine how much needs to be taken out. And yes, insurance companies do follow-up after surgery to ensure the correct amount was taken out, and if not, they will deny the claim.

Dr. Johnson stated that his experience with Aetna is that they DOUBLE the Schnurr Scale numbers, and therefore, very few people are approved. And if they are approved, the surgeon has to remove a dramatic amount of breast tissue and could make the patient much smaller than she wants to be. Your surgeon should be able to tell you if yours will likely be covered.

FINANCIAL COST

Insurance companies also require long-term documentation of back pain and under breast sores. If these issues are not properly documented, your surgery could be denied.

I spoke to several surgeon's offices on my quest to find a surgeon, and most did not accept insurance. I asked them why. Many stated that in the past, they had gone to great lengths to document the need for a patient's breast reduction, and several had been approved. The surgeon's offices reported that they then performed the surgery utilizing the operating room, all the nurses, the anesthesiologist, medical assistants, and all of their talents and efforts only to have the entire claim denied after the fact. Can you imagine what a mess that caused for everyone involved?

I decided that I wanted the best surgeon I could find, and I didn't want to wait months or even years before having my procedure. (I was 56 years old and felt I had waited long enough!) But some others have been very successful having insurance cover their surgeries.

Chris described her experience:

I began by complaining of back pain and rashes under the breast to my primary [doctor]. Then I saw an orthopedist, chiropractor, pain management doctor and went to PT to build my case for insurance. I don't know what they required, but I refused to be turned away...I consulted with a surgeon and had all those doctors write letters to the insurance. They approved me very quickly. Not saying everyone has to jump through these hoops but I was not taking no for an answer...

Q: How much does surgery cost out of pocket?

I live near Phoenix, Arizona and had my surgery in June 2024. With all of the fees including anesthesia, operating room, medical staff, and most supplies, my cost was approximately $12,000. I consider this a very reasonable price, but I did not have that kind of money lying around.

I spoke to several other women about the cost of their surgeries, and I noticed that prices do vary. You can call several surgeon's offices and they will likely give you general figure of how much a patient could expect to pay for a breast reduction, but that figure will be on the low side. You will know the exact price of your surgery only after the consultation.

Jenavieve said

Insurance wouldn't cover mine so I paid 100% out of pocket. My total was $8,800 and that included post op appointments.

Amanda stated

I paid for all mine out of pocket. It was like $10,800.

In doing my research and speaking to many women in Canada and the UK, paying out of pocket for the surgery is much more affordable than in the US.

Q: How could you afford it?

Luckily, I had good credit, so I decided to finance my surgery. Most plastic surgeons accept Care Credit, which is a credit card that can be used for various medical procedures such as dental work and plastic surgery. Just go to carecredit.com and give it a shot. I was able to make large payments every month until it was paid off within a year, and I paid no interest whatsoever.

*(Other options I considered were credit cards, tapping into my 401, or waiting until I saved up the cash. I was feeling pretty desperate, so I wanted to move quickly.)

Canada and the UK

In order to have a breast reduction covered by public healthcare, patients typically start by consulting their primary physician who assesses symptoms such as chronic pain in the neck, shoulders, and back, skin irritation, or posture problems. If your breast reduction is shown to be medically necessary, the primary doctor refers you to a specialist such as a plastic surgeon who further evaluates your case.

Oftentimes, the healthcare system requires proof that physical therapy or weight loss have not solved the above listed problems. The plastic surgeon then submits a request to the appropriate government health agency for approval.

6

TIME OFF WORK/SCHOOL

Son, if you really want something in this life, you have to work for it. *Now quiet! They're about to announce the lottery numbers.*
-Homer Simpson

If you have a job, you may not want to take a lot of time off work. You may not have enough PTO or vacation time and wonder if you can just take off a couple of weeks at most.

Different women respond to surgery differently. I have talked to women who have gone back to work within two weeks with few restrictions. (I believe these women to be smiled upon by the breast reduction gods!) Most women, like myself, need to take off at least six full weeks for a smooth recovery. I know this sounds like a lot, but believe me, I needed every single day of that six weeks.

I have talked to a lot of women, and the recovery times vary. My experience was exactly like many other women I've talked to, and Rosa said it so well when talking about her own recovery:

I am one of those whose recovery is taking much longer than average. I didn't have serious complications...[but] I have barely left the house since surgery. I will be 6 weeks post op tomorrow and only this past week I've felt I started turning a corner in terms of pain and soreness. I'm still not driving, and walks make me more sore, so I'm still resting mostly. But I am now able to comfortably shower and do my hair every day, water my plants, do some light cooking and tidying up...I have started to have very good days and I'm in a good mood ever since I accepted the fact that my body needs more time and rest than other women to heal and that doesn't mean there's something wrong with me.

And I spoke to Ann, and she said this:

My doctor wrote a note for 8 weeks! I have a physical job with a lot of standing, lifting and bending. No way I could do it earlier than 8 weeks.

The advice I got from Chloe was this:

My only tip is please don't rush through your recovery, EVEN when the initial pain has subsided and you're feeling "up to it." There is no prize for rushing back into work, driving, the gym, etc. before you're ready... all that does is compromise your own healing. I know not all of us have a choice (i.e. no childcare/no family help) but for us lucky ladies that do... sit down and stay down PLEASE."

Q: Did you really have to wait six whole weeks?

When I first scheduled my surgery, I took six weeks off work because my surgeon recommended that. I used FMLA and short-term disability and had it all pre-approved. However, I thought that it would be possible to return to work early. I even told my boss that after the third week, I might come back to work. I did not.

Q: Doesn't it depend on what kind of work you do?

For me, I'm blessed to work from home. Even with that significant advantage, I was truly not well enough to work for a solid six weeks.

I have spoken to many women after their breast reduction surgeries, and I've been surprised to find out that some people do go back to work after only two or three weeks, and have very little pain after surgery. You might be one of the lucky ones who achieves these kinds of results.

The pain and limitations lingered on for me. Dr. Johnson was able to make my breasts as small as I wanted which meant removing a lot of tissue and moving a lot of things around. When I felt frustrated that my recovery was taking longer than I was hoping, I reminded myself that my body underwent major surgery. The body is miraculous in how it can heal itself, but it does need time.

Q: Will my surgeon be able to tell me exactly how long I should be out of work?

Not exactly. Your surgeon can estimate the time you will need but will not be able to tell if you will be one of the lucky ones whose pain is low and healing is fast. This will depend on what happens in the operating room, your tolerance for pain, and how well you care for yourself afterward.

Q: I've had surgery before and healed quickly. Would that be a good sign for this surgery?

Yes. If you have undergone major surgery before on any part of your body, you can probably get a basic idea of how you will react to surgery.

TIME OFF WORK/SCHOOL

For example, you'll know if you tolerate anesthesia well. You'll know if you healed more quickly than expected before, or if you took the allotted time to heal. I knew from my past hysterectomy and my past ankle surgery that I heal at about the average rate.

My advice is to be safe and take off at least six weeks. If you have a physical job, I would take eight weeks. If you end up being one of the lucky ones, you can always go back to work or school earlier than you planned.

7

YOUR SUPPORT SYSTEM

Friendship is so weird…You just pick a human you've met and you're like "Yep, I like this one" and you just do stuff with them.
-Anonymous

Before your surgery, you will need to tap into your support system. At the very least, you will need someone to drive you to and from surgery. A responsible hospital or surgical center will not release you to a taxi, Lyft or Uber driver. I also needed a driver for the first two appointments. At home, I needed support from my husband.

Q: My husband is not the best nurse. How much will I need him?

I understand that. My husband is a rough and tumble redneck who's always got a tool in his hand and a knife in his pocket. I was not sure how much I could depend on him for gentle care after surgery. But he surprised me.

My husband, Mike, took time off work to be there for me on the first two days and for my first appointment. I needed him to help me into and out of bed, and to just observe me to make sure there were no emergencies. Over the weeks, he really stepped up.

I was one of the lucky ones. Even though he was working, he would still make meals, tidy up the house, take care of the dogs, and sometimes bring me things so I didn't have to get up. He also made sure I had my hands on the remote control. I was so pleasantly surprised by his level of support.

I checked in with others, and Suzanne L said:
  ...My husband has been a life saver! I'm two weeks post op and still need his help for at least 80%

I also heard from Shauna:
  I...very much needed help getting dressed, showering, brushing my hair, & I could barely wipe myself. Hang in there, it gets better.

Erin had great advice for Shauna when she said:
  There are cheap bidets on Amazon you can install on your toilet seat for $30 ish. As long as you have someone who can help install it, it would help with getting clean "down there" when your reach is limited.

Q: What if I don't have anyone to help me?

If you prepare your house, pre-prepare some snacks and easy meals, have all your medications filled and on-hand, and have your phone nearby, you could conceivably do this on your own after the first day. It might be a rough journey without any help, but it can be done. I recommend you check in with a friend daily, through text or calls, so that if anything complications arise or you need a ride to the doctor's office, she is there to help.

Q: What if I have small children to care for?

This is again where I recommend that you tap into your support system because you most likely will need some help. It will be difficult to pick them up or bathe them for at least a few weeks.

I know it's not easy to ask for help.

Denise explained this very well on social media:
I'm 9 days post-op and I'm so frustrated about not having my independence. I think I have been healing well and able to do some things, but I hate having to ask for help and not being able to do things my way... I'm so uncomfortable if something isn't done the way I would do it...I'm also feeling guilty for needing help, like I am a burden.

Jill had an excellent idea to find extra help:
Any chance u can afford to hire a care aid for 2 hrs a day, even for days 3-6 to pick up any slack & to ease your load/worries?.. I believe it would be approximately $50 to have someone come for a few hours a day...if nothing else, to cook, clean, help kids, whatever. It sounds like a luxury but may ease your load immensely.

My advice is find someone to assist you, at least for the first few days. If you have a partner, let them know you'll be needing them for a while so they can prepare to step up. I needed my husband's help less and less, but I was so grateful he was there for the tough days.

8

GATHER YOUR SUPPLIES

*I've had so much plastic surgery,
when I die they will donate my body to Tupperware.*
-Joan Rivers

I learned so much about what items can make the recovery process easier. Don't worry, you **don't** need to buy everything on this list. This is just a list of possible supplies and options. I will bold the ones that I found most helpful:

- **Mastectomy pillow** – This was my most important purchase, and I got mine from Amazon. It's a soft, protective pillow that you wear across the front of your breasts, with side pillows for the sides of your breasts. It has an adjustable strap that secures in the back so you can wear it and walk around with it on. I have small dogs that jump on me when I'm in my recliner, and this pillow protected me from getting injured. It also protected me from the seat belt when I rode in the car.

- Wedge pillow – Immediately after your surgery, you will need to sleep on your back and as upright as possible. This is so the breasts heal evenly and in the desired position. And side sleeping is way too painful at first. A lot of women are just like me in the sense that I do NOT like sleeping on my back. But the wedge pillow made it easier and more comfortable. I could have done without the wedge pillow if I had enough pillows on my bed to create the wedge effect.

- Pregnancy pillow – Many women get this instead of the wedge pillow. It is a long, U-shaped pillow that can prop up your torso. It can later be used for support when you start side sleeping.

- Neck pillow – Some women have found that a neck pillow really helped with their comfort levels. I didn't use one, but I kinda wish I had. It would go great with either a wedge pillow or a pregnancy pillow.

- Pillow with a back rest – I searched on Amazon for "back support pillow." I didn't use this but several women have recommended it.

- **Basket** – Yes, I am suggesting you get yourself a basket with a handle. I have advised many women to do this, and they all proclaimed it was a great idea. A basket can hold all of the essentials that you need to keep with you so you don't have to get up and down too often. You can carry it all with you when you change locations in the house, from the bed to the couch or recliner, and vice versa. Here are some of the things I kept in my basket:

- Pain meds and antibiotics
- 2-3 bottles of water (VERY important to stay hydrated)
- Reading glasses
- A couple of protein bars
- A couple of snacks like pretzels and trail mix
- My phone
- A book

- Keep a trash can nearby – you don't want to get up and down every time you have to throw something away.

- Front closing pajamas and tops – For several weeks, you won't be able to raise your arms over your head. The pajamas I got from Amazon are perfect! You can get any brand, but I got Ekouaer Nightgowns in a two pack. These types of pajamas can be found almost anywhere such as Walmart or Target.

- Maxi-pads or panty liners – I had a hysterectomy years ago, so I did not want to buy these. But trust me, if you are leaking a little bit of blood from your incisions, pads and panty liners are much softer against your skin than gauze. The slight difference does matter when you're experiencing post-surgical pain.

- **Stool softener or laxatives** – One of the top complaints about surgery in general is constipation. Anesthesia, pain medication, and lack of movement are all contributors. Don't just sit there getting backed up. Do something about it by drinking a lot of water and taking stool softeners or laxatives.

- Bras – It may be difficult to hold yourself back, but wait until after surgery to buy any bras. You won't know your exact size until it's done. We will talk about bras at length in later chapters.

You will also need to have some easy to make meals on hand. Sometimes you might not feel like eating, but I stayed on a regular schedule of eating breakfast, lunch and dinner which helped my stomach tolerate the medications. These items made it easy to care for myself when my husband was at work.

- Healthy Choice Steamers frozen meals were my favorite! They have a lot of vegetables in them, are low calorie, and taste fresh and delicious. They are so much better than other frozen meals, in my opinion.
- Protein bars and shakes – these really came in handy when I didn't feel much like eating but I knew I needed to.
- High protein cereal

- Greek Yogurt
- Cottage cheese with toppings. I topped with fruit such as blueberries, bananas, or strawberries. If I was out of fruit, I topped cottage cheese with salad toppers. You can buy a small bag of salad toppers that include things like pecans, cranberries, seeds and other nuts.
- Tuna – You can get tuna in small pouches that are already made into different types of tuna salads. You can just scoop them onto bread or eat it with crackers. It wouldn't require any chopping or mixing.
- Snacks such as pretzels, cashews or trail mix.
- You can prepare frozen meals ahead of time and keep them handy.

Gather the supplies that work for you, and have them ready the day of surgery. Preparation is key to your comfort after surgery.

9

BEFORE PHOTOS

I'm glad I've got boobs.
The last thing I need is someone making eye contact with me.
-Unknown

If you're anything like me, I didn't like having my picture taken. I didn't have a ton of photos of my "before" breasts, so take my advice: now is the time to take some pictures. You will want them after the surgery to compare to your results.

According to Ashley on social media:
   Heads up if you HAVE NOT had surgery yet. DO make sure you take photos of yourself in a few of your tops that you love before going to surgery! I have major regret for not doing so. Most of my photos are neck/chest up and I can't really get a good comparison in clothing.

Antonia responded with:

BEFORE PHOTOS

Same here! I didn't even realize until after surgery. I took 1 photo the night before & that's all I have...

Here is my one before photo:

Besides photos, one of the things I did became an excellent way of comparing my before and after. You should try it.

Get a basic cheap white tee shirt and put it on without your bra. Take a sharpie and, drawing on the tee shirt, outline your breasts in their natural position. Be sure to draw a circle where your nipple lies. After the surgery, you can put on the tee shirt and draw lines around your new breasts and a circle around your new nipples. You will really see a difference!

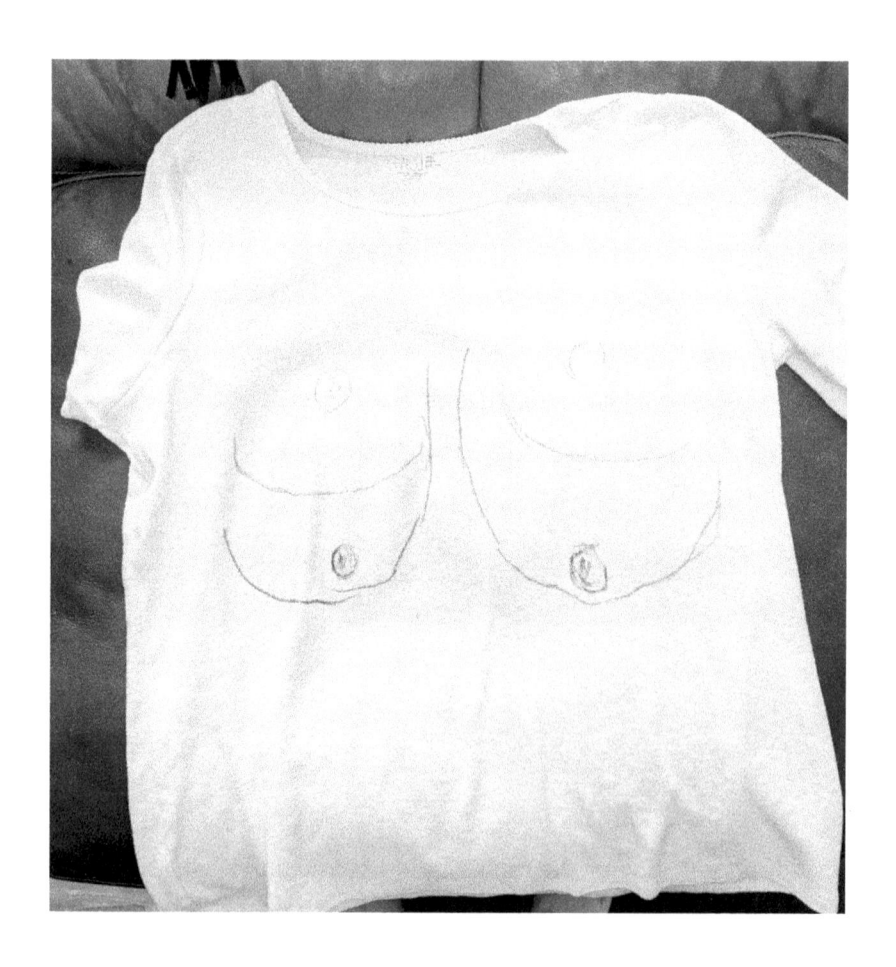

10

FOLLOWING INSTRUCTIONS

Wherever the art of medicine is loved, there is also a love of humanity.
                                -Hippocrates

Before we go forward, I want to take a moment to advise you to follow all the surgeon's instructions prior to surgery. I know this sounds obvious, and I am a good little rule follower, but let me tell you what happened with my case so this won't happen to you.

I got the surgery scheduled and waited patiently for my surgery date. I had a list of presurgical instructions, and one of the instructions was to stop taking certain medications such as fish oil, blood thinners, or semaglutide medications such as Ozempic.

I was very wary of stopping Ozempic because I was worried I would gain weight back. But the doctor explained I need to stop it for a week to ten days because the medication slows down how quickly food is processed in the stomach. There was a risk that I could vomit with the tube down my throat which could cause serious health issues. With that advice, I stopped taking Ozempic for ten days prior to surgery.

I had been fasting the day before surgery, just to be sure. Since I had no food in my stomach, I decided to go ahead and take my Ozempic the night before.

I went to the surgical center the day of surgery so very nervous and excited.

In the surgical center, the medical assistants completely prepared me for surgery and just as I was about to be taken into the operating room, the anesthesiologist came to talk to me. She asked a series of important presurgical questions and one of them was, "When was the last time you took your Ozempic?" And I replied, "Last night, after I had been fasting." In what felt like a nightmare at the time, my surgery was cancelled on the spot! I was mortified!

I learned that even with no food in my stomach, it could still cause a back-up in my stomach during surgery. She explained that if that happened, I could possibly suffocate and die. It's so scary to think that if I had held this information back, I could have had major complications or could have even died. At the time that it happened, I was shocked, upset, and angry at myself. I had to call my husband and tell him to come back and pick me up.

I was lucky that Dr. Johnson had a surgery cancellation that was set in the very near future, and his office gave me that slot. I was able to have a second chance for surgery. I also consider myself blessed that I was not charged extra for any of this. (I felt so guilty, I would have paid it.)

FOLLOWING INSTRUCTIONS

Please learn from my mistake and follow all instructions. If you have a question about your instructions, please call your surgeon's office and ask before you do something that could cause your surgery to be cancelled and delayed.

11

PREPARING YOURSELF

I believe that people make their own luck by great preparation and good strategy.
-Jack Canfield

This is the point where you need to prepare yourself for surgery. I suggest you fill all your medications prior to surgery, if you can. You may be someone who doesn't like to take medications or who is worried about addiction to opioids. My suggestion is to fill the prescription anyway. You might need it more than you think.

Pain levels very greatly, but I was in some pretty significant pain afterward. I took my prescribed pain medication and even got a much needed refill on the meds. However, pain medications can only be given for a very short time in order to avoid addiction. If you find that after your surgery, you don't really need pain medication, then you don't have to take it. (And I am also extremely jealous.)

I dealt with a lot of pre-surgical anxiety. I wondered what I would end up looking like and hoped like hell I could deal with the pain. I checked and rechecked my list of supplies. I also went on social media and found support. You can find many breast reduction support groups online where you can talk about how you feel. You will get support and advice from some amazing women, just like I did. I do want to caution you that these groups sometimes bring out the extremes. You will read horror stories and stories of women who went back to work in a week. Remember that the average patient heals well within 6-8 weeks.

The Night Before

Because you'll be under general anesthesia, you will need to stop eating at a certain time the night before. Your surgeon's office will give you exact instructions. Since my surgery was first thing in the morning, I had to stop eating and drinking around 8pm the night before.

Dr. Johnson's instructions were to take a shower the night before with antibacterial soap (I chose Dial antibacterial bar soap) and then to shower again the morning of surgery. After showering, DO NOT put on any type of deodorant, lotion, or powder. The body needs to be very clean to help prevent infection.

Get a good night's sleep. It's common to feel excitement and anxiety the night before surgery. You'll be worrying about all of the unknowns and wondering what the pain will feel like. That's normal. Do your best to clear your mind and relax. Remember that you are in good hands with your surgical team, and that they perform this surgery all the time. It's a first for you, but it's not their first rodeo. Trust that you made the right decision for your health and well-being, and know that the results will be worth it all. So lay your head down and allow yourself some peace.

Positive Mindset

Having a positive mindset can actually make a difference in your recovery experience. According to Elizabeth Perry, ACC, in an article called "Improve your life with a new outlook: 10 benefits of positive thinking," the author acknowledges that when we feel frustrated, sad, or afraid, it's ok to spend some time with those negative feelings. The key is to acknowledge them, then move on.

She states that hope and growth are good for your wellness, and she provides a list of the benefits of positive thinking.
- Better stress management and coping skills during stressful moments
- Lower risk of depression
- More resistant to the common cold and a stronger immune system
- Decreased risk of heart attacks and heart disease
- Lower blood pressure
- Better problem-solving
- Greater ability to adapt to change
- More creative thinking
- Consistent attitude with fewer mood swings
- Stronger leadership skills

I found some excellent advice on how to switch a negative mindset to a positive one. Here are the suggestions that worked very well for me.

- Mental rehearsal – Imagine yourself at the surgery center or hospital. Visualize everything going very smoothly in every detail. Imagine waking up, feeling heavy and tired, and imagine the relief of going home and slipping into your bed. Visualize yourself

comfortably healing.
- Goals visualization – Visualize yourself healed up after surgery. Imagine how much lighter you will feel, how fun it will be to buy new clothes, and how much more balanced you will look. Keep those images in your mind and allow yourself to feel the joy.

Q: What if I'm still anxious?

I found it helpful to listen to a guided meditation on youtube.com. My favorite one is called "A Havening Guided Meditation to Reduce Health Anxiety" by Dr. Kate Truitt. If you don't want to listen to a guided meditation, then I suggest mindful breathing techniques for anxiety. I am a subscriber to the YouTube channel called Therapy in a Nutshell, and the breathing techniques I've learned have been of tremendous benefit to me over the years.

According to therapist Emma McAdam, anxiety occurs when your autonomic nervous system is activated by a real or perceived threat. We don't directly control our autonomic nervous system, so just saying to yourself "calm down" will probably not work. How can you use breathing to turn down the anxiety response? Emma McAdam gave some fantastic advice that helped me relax before surgery.

First just explore your breath by putting one hand on your chest and one hand on your stomach and breathe as you would normally breathe. What do you notice? Which hand moves? For many, the shoulders lift or the chest rises, but their stomachs are tight.

Now inhale deeply and hold your breath for a few seconds, then let out a sigh. Do it again. This is a natural tension release, which you might notice yourself doing when you feel frustrated or upset.

Find your pulse on your wrist. Pay attention to your breath and slow down your breathing. Breathe in for 4 seconds and breathe out for 4 seconds. Close your eyes. Breathe in for 4 seconds, hold for 4 seconds, and breathe out slowly for 5 seconds. Do it again. Did you notice what happened to your heart rate? Long, slow outbreaths slow your heart rate and sends your mind messages to calm down.

Emma also suggests slow Belly Breathing. Lie flat on your back or sit in a comfortable chair. Place one hand on your chest and one hand on your stomach. Can you allow your stomach to raise first? Feel the difference when you breathe with your stomach expanding instead of breathing with your chest. Breathe in 4-5 seconds, hold 4 seconds, and let it out for 5 seconds. Just find the right pace. You want your breathing to be slow, smooth, and steady. Relax your shoulders and allow your stomach to rise.

You can make space for your feelings. Anxiety won't kill you. According to the New York Times, conscious breathing exercises can bring a lot of benefits such as reducing blood pressure, regulating your heart rate, and lifting your mood. Researchers have also reported that breathing slowly can reduce chronic pain, stress and depression.

Affirmations helped me greatly when my mind was spiraling and worrying. Examples of positive affirmations include such things as:

- *I am relaxed and calm as I prepare for this surgery.*
- *I have an excellent surgeon who will take great care of me.*
- *I will wake up after surgery and my pain will be well-managed*
- *Thousands, if not millions, of women do this every year. If they can do it,*

I can do it.
- *I am strong and resilient. I am prepared for this surgery.*

Once you get into the operating room, your surgeon has control. But as soon as you get home, your recovery is in your hands. The more prepared you can be, physically and mentally, the smoother your recovery will be.

II

Part Two

There's pure joy in moving forward with your transformation, shedding the weight of doubt and stepping into your new self. Like a butterfly emerging from its cocoon, each step you take will bring newfound confidence, strength, and a sense of rebirth. You are ready, and the time is now to step forward into your radiant and beautifully balanced new body.

12

THE DAY OF SURGERY

Change your life today. Don't gamble on the future, act now, without delay.
  -Simone de Beauvoir

This is the day I'd been waiting for, so I woke up both excited and extremely nervous. Even as I got ready, I continued consciously breathing slowly and repeating my affirmations. I bathed with the antibacterial soap and then put on my button-front night gown and slippers. I didn't bother to wear a bra. I was not concerned with how I looked; I only cared how comfortable I would be after the procedure.

Before I left the house, I made sure my wedge pillow was in place on the bed, my basket was stocked with my side table supplies, and I had my pain medication and antibiotics filled and ready. I also took some things I needed out of my upper cabinets and put them on lower shelves, knowing I'd have difficulty reaching upwards after the surgery. I brought my mastectomy pillow in the car.

Now it was time to go. My advice: Leave in plenty of time for check in. Since I was already nervous, running late would have created more anxiety than I would ever want.

The ride to the surgical center felt like it took forever. It was hard to contain my excitement, and I just kept visualizing how it would feel and look to have more modest breasts. I arrived at the surgical center in plenty of time and checked in, and they called me back. Dr. Johnson advised that the surgery should take approximately four hours, so I sent my husband off to go shopping or get something to eat. The assistants guided me to a bed with a big curtain around it and had me undress completely. I put on the front opening paper gown and socks they gave me. They also gave me a surgical cap to put on to hold all my hair. I then lay down on the bed. The surgery center felt cold to me, and the nurse kindly covered me in a warm blanket.

The nurse then came with a clipboard and went down a checklist of questions. She asked if I had followed all pre-surgical instructions and made sure I had stopped taking Ozempic for at least a week prior to surgery. I had done exactly as instructed this time.

Next, the nurse inserted an IV into a vein on the back of my hand. I then lay in the bed waiting for the surgeon and anesthesiologist to come and speak to me. It felt like this all took a long time because I was so incredibly eager to get this over with. I watched the clock like a hawk.

Dr. Johnson arrived looking fresh and ready, and he had me stand up with my arms at my sides. He opened my gown and used a purple marker to draw marks all over my chest and breasts. I stood perfectly still with good posture. This all felt a little weird and took about 15 minutes. I felt my excitement building that this was really happening… FINALLY.

THE DAY OF SURGERY

This was the beginning of my transformation.

When the surgeon finished drawing on me, he left to prepare himself for surgery. Then the anesthesiologist came and spoke with me. He went down his list of questions, and I was cleared for surgery. Here we go!

When it was finally time, I walked into the operating room with a nurse escorting me and carrying my IV. The team helped me lie down on the operating table. I didn't really have time to look around the operating room, but I do remember seeing the anesthesiologist, the surgeon, and at least one surgical assistant.

They had me position my arms in a certain way, kind of out to the sides. And then, that is literally the last thing I remember. Once I was positioned, the anesthesia immediately started. I was out like a light.

I felt like I was asleep for about five minutes when I woke up, but they told me the procedure was done. Everything went very well, they told me, but Dr. Johnson had to make the incisions on my sides a bit longer than planned. Because of this, I had more sutures than they originally thought I would need. I understood everything they told me about how it went, even though I was still pretty groggy. They told me I had stayed asleep for about two hours after the procedure. I did not remember any of that.

The nurse helped me sit up. My chest felt so heavy, like an elephant was sitting on my sternum. It was hard to take a deep breath. She helped me into my button front pajama dress, and it was then I realized the brilliance of the wardrobe choice. I was so thankful I didn't have to raise my arms.

I looked down, and I saw that I was wearing a tight compression bra. I could see blood on the white bandages underneath. The doctor had already explained that it's normal to have some light bleeding or seepage right after surgery.

After I was dressed, they brought my husband in to see me. This is a memory that always makes me laugh. He had his phone and immediately took pictures of me. He exclaimed, "Oh my gosh! Look how flat chested you are!" I still look back on that comment and find it hilarious. I have never been referred to as "flat chested" since I was 11 years old.

Q: Oh my gosh, did you really look flat chested? I don't want to be flat!

Dr. Johnson was able to reduce the size of my breasts to the level that I wanted while keeping the nipples alive and well. But at first, right after surgery, my new smaller breasts were pressed tightly to my chest with the compression bra. My first impression was that I really did appear flat, but later, when I took off the compression bra, I was able to really see the results. I was definitely smaller, but I was not flat.

Q: Did you have drains?

Dr. Johnson explained that he would not know whether or not I needed drains until the surgery was complete and he would see how much fluid/blood I was producing. He did not want too much fluid to build up in my chest. Lucky for me, I did not need them. I have spoken to a lot of women who had drains and, in many cases, drains are necessary.

Drains are thin, flexible tubes approximately 14-18 inches long inserted into an opening in the soft tissues of the breast or armpit area. The tube has a soft plastic bulb on the end which creates a gentle suction to pull the fluid out of the body.

This excess fluid, called serous fluid, is a mixture of blood and lymph fluid. If this fluid is allowed to accumulate in the breast, it can cause bruising, discomfort, and infections. The drain tubes are secured with stitches and remain in place for approximately 3-10 days.(Be careful not to catch your tubing on anything because it can pull the tubing out.)

You will notice that the surgical team secured the drains onto your surgical bra with safety pins. The surgeon will give you specific instructions on how to care for your drains, and will likely be the following:
- Wash your hands before emptying the drain
- Empty drains into the toilet when they come half full.
- Rinse the empty bulb with water
- Gently compress the bulb to create a vacuum.
- Close the tubing system by attaching the bulb to the tubing.
- Keep the areas clean and dry
- Observe the drains and alert your physician's office if the color or consistency of the fluid changes

According to an article by the University of Utah regarding drains, when observing the drainage fluid, you should see the fluid changing consistency and color over time. You should observe the following progression:

1. Thick blood
2. Thin and red, like cranberry juice
3. Beige or slightly yellow, like the color of straw
4. Clear

You must be aware of any signs of infection. If you observe any fluid that is creamy or milky, or you notice any of the following signs, call your surgeon's office right away.(Your doctor will be on-call for these issues.)

- A fever of 101 degrees F or higher
- Redness around the drain site
- Increasing pain at the drain site
- Hardness near the drain site
- Thickening of the drainage fluid (it should be thinning over time)
- Swelling of the surgical area
- Foul-smelling drainage fluid

Q: How long does it take for a drain hole to heal?

The hole should close in just a few days. The drainage hole is pretty small, less than the size of a dime, and should take 3-4 weeks to fully heal.

GOING HOME

There's no place like home. There's no place like home.
-Dorothy in The Wizard of Oz

I had my surgery at a surgical center, and then I was released to go home after I woke up. At the car, my husband helped me put on my mastectomy pillow and secure it in the back. He helped me into my seat, slightly reclined my seat, and secured my seat belt. The pillow did its job beautifully, and the seat belt did not hurt me at all.I was relaxed and felt exhausted.I could feel that my body had just been through a lot. For the ride, I just rested my eyes. I was sore and tender, and was especially thankful that my husband drove very carefully.

13

THE FIRST WEEK

> Healing is the application of love to the places inside that hurt.
> -Iyanla Vanzant

On the first day, I slept a lot and took my pain medication every four hours. I also took my antibiotics on schedule. I got comfortable in bed, had my basket of supplies on hand, and had my mastectomy pillow on at all times. (My dogs wanted to be all over me and sniff me. To them, I smelled so weird!) Later in the day, I decided to get out of bed and rest in my recliner. I needed my husband to help me up, and I needed his arm for support the first time walking to the den.

Q: What was the pain like?

My entire chest and every inch of my breasts were throbbing. I felt intense pressure on my chest, especially on the sternum between my breasts. I was so tender! My nipples were extremely sensitive, and I got frequent "zingers."

Q: What is a "zinger"?

A zinger is a sudden pain that shoots through your breasts and feels like an electric shock. I remember cursing the first few times I felt it. Zingers happen because the nerve endings have been cut and are now trying to heal themselves. One surgeon described it as "the nerve endings trying to find their friends." This is good news! Zingers are actually a very positive sign that your sensation is returning. My surgeon advised that even years later, I could feel a zinger once in a while.

The pain from a breast reduction surgery varies from person to person, but it's generally described as a deep aching soreness combined with surface tenderness. The chest feels tight and swollen with a pulling or burning sensation around the incisions.

The pain killers worked really well that first week. I felt weak as a kitten and was constantly aware of the tremendous pressure on my chest. I felt like I was wearing a bra that was too tight.

Dr. Johnson's office called me the day after surgery to check on me. They asked me detailed questions about my level of pain and bleeding. I told them that I was no longer bleeding, but that it felt like the bra was too tight. (Good communication is key!) They advised that I could cut the compression bra they gave me in a couple of places along the band. It loosened up just enough to feel comfortable. What a relief!

Q: Don't they give you a bra that fits right?

First of all, the bra they give you after surgery is not magic. It's just a basic compression bra and it's supposed to be tight. But I am a plus sized girl and sometimes an XL can be a bit too tight. Once I put some slits in the band, it was perfect. My surgeon advised me to wear the compression bra day and night until further notice.

Q: I'm dying to know…how did your breasts look?

When I took off my compression bra, I saw that I was covered in gauze and tape. In the mirror, I looked at myself from the front and sides. I saw that on the sides of my body, near the arm pits, I was remarkably bruised from the laser liposuction that I opted to add to my surgery. I also noticed butterfly sutures on my incisions under the bandages. I took some selfies. And to be honest, I kept peeking down at my breasts every chance I got. It took a while to wrap my mind around the new size.

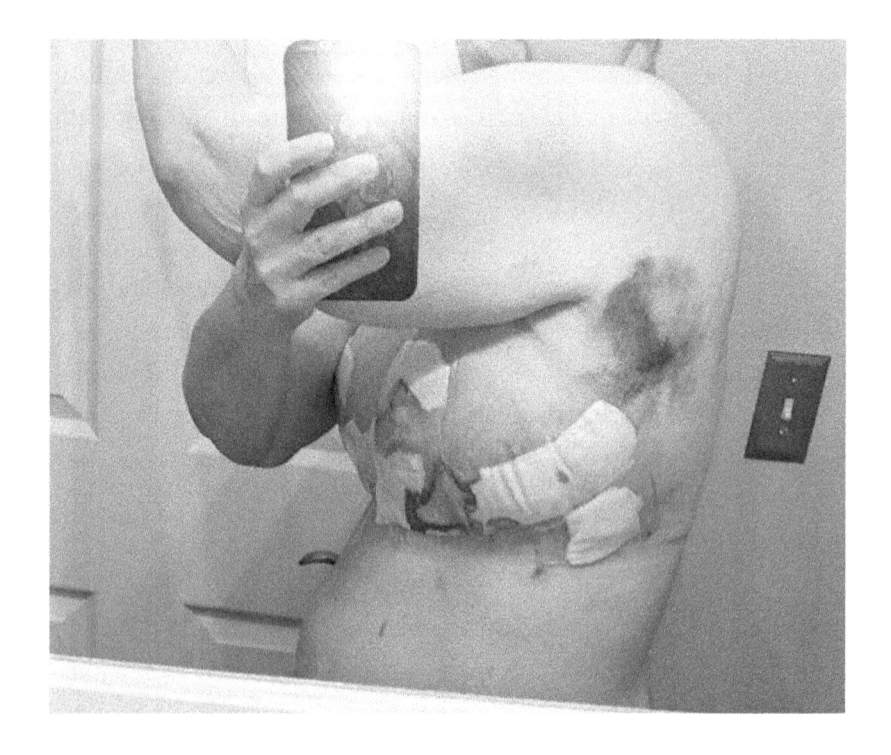

THE FIRST WEEK

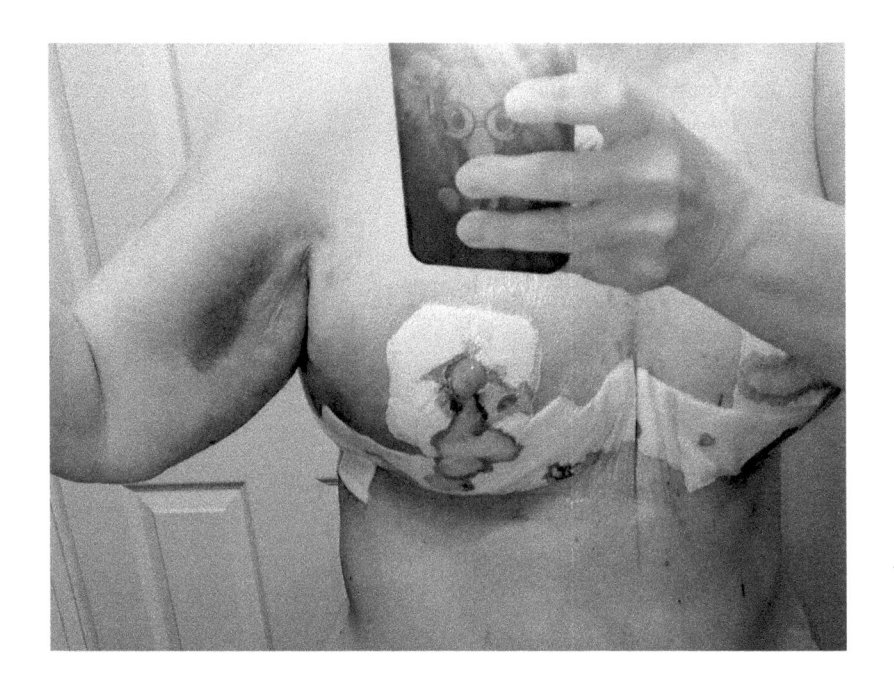

Q: Was it the size you wanted?

At first, I thought I was too small. My breasts were high and tight, and there was some fluid gurgling around in my chest. (Remember that I did not have drains.) I could feel and hear the fluid move when I pressed my fingers on my chest.

A few days after surgery, I found myself so concerned about my small size that I was in tears. I thought to myself, "What did I do?!" Suddenly, I felt a great sense of loss and like less of a woman. I talked to many women who had had the surgery, and they all said this is a normal reaction. I was so used to my breasts being big and heavy, that actually being more balanced felt strange at first.

Showering

The gauze, tape and the butterfly sutures need to stay on and remain dry, so getting right into a shower is not a good idea. Dr. Johnson told me that I could shower if I turned away from the water, and he explained that if the butterfly sutures get moist, they can get gooey and that could prevent healing in that area. I did not want to risk my incisions opening up, so this is what I opted to do:

I turned on the water for the bathtub. I sat on the edge of the tub and used a carefully rung out wash cloth to wash my arm pits. I then washed the parts below my waist unhindered. When I washed my hair, I sat on my knees at the side of the tub and used a cup to wet and wash my hair.

These may sound like extreme measures. I reasoned that I paid a lot of money for this surgery, and I wanted the best results, so I avoided getting any water on my breasts.This is exactly the way I bathed until the butterfly sutures came off. But I spoke to many other women who had different experiences.

Connie stated:
 While using T-rex arms, I showered by myself on day 5, the day I got my drains out, with the water on my back. Had my husband on hand within yelling distance but had no issues.Everyone is different.

Deanna said the following:
 My surgeon told me only sponge baths for the first 5 days, then once he removed the bandages I could shower. I needed help the first shower, but after

that I just tried as much as I could.

And Kayla said:
  Maybe I'm an exception, but I was showering alone day 4.My husband was here in case I got dizzy like I did the first shower..."

Q: Could you use deodorant?

Thankfully, yes. But I was very swollen and sore in the area, so I applied it gingerly, being careful to avoid the incisions.

Q: What is wound breakdown?

During your recovery, you will need to check your sutures periodically to ensure your wounds are still closed and healing.Some causes of wound breakdown include obesity, smoking, and poor diet. If you notice your wounds appear to be opening up or breaking down, call your surgeon's office immediately. They will want to see you in the office, observe your wounds, and will recommend a treatment for wound breakdown. Treatment normally involves topical ointment and gauze or pads. Dressings will need to be changed daily after bathing.

Back sleeping

Sleeping on my back was difficult at first because I'm a side sleeper. But of course, I wanted to heal evenly so I followed instructions and slept on my back and slightly upright using the wedge pillow. Some women use a CPAP machine and have extra difficulty sleeping on their backs.

Terry asked:
  Are any of you side sleepers who uses a CPAP machine?... tried to sleep on

my back but my mask couldn't maintain a good seal in that position, so I couldn't sleep well and was EXHAUSTED.

Kim quickly chimed in to help her:

I am a Respiratory Therapist. Get the incline pillow system. It's adjustable and has leg booster that helps keep your body position. Also a pregnancy pillow... Trust me on this one!! Both on Amazon.

Helen was also helpful when she said:

I find the key for me is to bring a bunch of the air hose across my body to the opposite side from the machine. If it just falls down between the bedside table and the bed, it will never maintain a good seal because of the downward pull. Bring the hose across you and then there isn't any pull on your mask.

Contacting your surgeon

I was advised to call Dr. Johnson's office immediately if I encountered any problems. In fact, he insisted I call him, even over the weekend or holiday, if I noticed any of the following:

- Excessive bleeding.
- An extreme increase in pain.
- If I saw any sutures open.
- If any area was extremely red or hot.
- If I had any other questions.

I was really impressed that my Dr. Johnson made himself available to me at all hours. I did not feel the need to call him, but it was a great comfort to know I could at any time.

At this point in my recovery, I did very little. I did nothing but watch tv and sleep that first week. I tried to use my laptop one day to get a few things done, but just reaching forward to tap on the keys was painful and draining. After about 15 minutes, I was exhausted and went back to sleep. Then, around the 6th or 7th day, I had my first follow up appointment.

The First Follow-up Appointment

I was excited to see Dr. Johnson for my first appointment. I wore a front buttoning top and my husband drove me to the office. Of course, I wore my mastectomy pillow in the car. I took my pain meds.

The doctor and his assistant came into the room and I undressed my torso. With gentle hands, the assistant removed all my blood-soaked gauze and tape. This took a few minutes because I was so sensitive that it still hurt a bit to pull the tape off my nipples and all my incisions. When it was done, it was a great relief.

Dr. Johnson examined my breasts and my incisions, still held together by the butterfly sutures, and he stated that everything was looking good. I was very swollen, especially on the sides where I had the laser liposuction. He explained that the swelling and bruising was normal, and the amount of fluid under my skin in my chest was also normal. I was healing well.

He sent me home with instructions to continue resting, do not get my breasts wet, and to take Tylenol for the pain. Dr. Johnson again insisted that I call if I noticed any type of problem or question. He stated he would rather I call and "bother" him than to allow a problem to fester and get worse.

14

THE SECOND WEEK

> *Our sorrow and wounds are healed only*
> *when we touch them with compassion.*
> -Jack Kornfield

I'm going to be honest: The second and third weeks were the most difficult. I had to remind myself that I had just been through major surgery, so the pain was part of the healing process. The pain medication had run out, and Tylenol barely made a dent. I complained a lot to my poor husband. However, I was pleased to notice that I could move around better and it was easier to get in and out of bed. I still slept partially upright on my back using the wedge pillow. I continued to eat regularly, shower carefully, and get lots of rest.

Q: What were your limitations?

Moving around was still pretty tough, especially if it involved my arms.

It was still difficult to reach upward, so opening cabinets to get a plate or a cup required assistance. If I did reach a little too far upward, I felt a sudden pain which I would describe as a ripping sensation under my breasts where the incisions were.

I followed another of Dr. Johnson's instructions: get up and walk around a little bit every day. I learned that blood circulation was extremely important for my healing. This did not mean to strap on my sneakers and go for a brisk walk around my neighborhood. (Oh no, I was not ready for THAT.) I just got up and walked around the house a little bit. I stepped out on my porch and walked around looking at the birds. That is about all I had the energy for.

The Second Follow-Up Appointment

In the second week, I had another follow-up appointment. I tapped into my support system, and my good friend Ann drove me because I was still too sore and weak to reach forward and turn the steering wheel.

The appointment went very similar to the first appointment, only this time the butterfly strips had to go. The surgeon's assistant came in first, and I removed my top for the examination. She began removing the strips, and this time it was a little bit more painful. Those things really stick! But again, her skilled and gentle touch made the removal much more bearable.

This was the first time I saw my breasts completely after surgery. I couldn't believe how perky they were, and how nicely the nipples faced forward. The suture lines were dark pink, which is normal for my complexion. I noticed that my areolas were much smaller, and my nipples seem to "fit" with my new smaller size. I was ecstatic, but deep down I still wondered if I was too small.

Dr. Johnson came into the room and examined me. I had a few visible stitches that he removed quickly with a snip snip. This did not really hurt much; it just felt like a tiny pinch. And he advised me that NOW I can take a proper shower.

I let him know that my breasts were extremely sensitive and I didn't even want to touch them. He advised that it would decrease my hyper-sensitivity to carefully wash my breasts in the shower and put body lotion on my chest (not the breasts). I was still significantly swollen, and he advised that the side area where I had the laser liposuction could be swollen for many months, or even up to a year. But the swelling in my breasts would subside in the coming weeks.

Q: What did the surgeon recommend for reducing the swelling?

Dr. Johnson had a couple of recommendations. (Do not do this until your surgeon tells you to.)
- Ice – I was to apply ice to my breasts for only 15 minutes at a time, being careful not to involve the nipples. The nipples were still healing and needed the blood flow to be unimpaired.
- Heat - I was then to apply heat for about 15 minutes, again avoiding the nipple. I used a heating pad, but you can use one of those rice bags that you heat up in the microwave.
- Lymph node draining techniques to help reduce the swelling. I had no idea what this was. The nurse explained that I could use my fingertips and very gently stroke the sides of my breasts toward the front of my body. It sort of felt like a tickle. As I got further along in my healing, I continued to drain my lymph nodes with this technique, and also added some gentle pressure so it felt like a bit

of a massage. You could even find a lymphatic drainage specialist, or a "Vodder" trained therapist in your area.
- Take Arnica. Several women I spoke with insisted that taking Arnica helped with their bruising and pain. This can be found on amazon in quick dissolving tablets that are gentle on the stomach.

Scars

Dr. Johnson then stated that it was time to start focusing on healing my scars, and he gave me options for scar treatment.

- Scar cream – He sold a pricey scar cream in his office, but I was not required to purchase it. It was just an option. This cream could be applied directly to the incisions.
- Scar tape – I bought some silicone scar tape from Amazon. I got the kind that is specifically made for breasts as it has a donut shaped piece that fits around the nipple incision, and then the anchor shaped piece that covers the scar going down the bottom of the breasts and extends to both sides under the breasts. The pieces fit perfectly on my body.

I chose the scar tape because it was easy. These pieces can be worn for 24 hours and just need to be removed for bathing. It's important to check your incisions periodically when first using the tape. You want to ensure that the silicone is not causing skin irritation that could make your incision worse. If it is, remove the tape immediately and speak to your surgeon's office.

Dr. Johnson also advised that while I was at home healing, I could remove all my upper clothing and just allow my breasts to be naked for a while. As long as I was protected by the mastectomy pillow and my dogs couldn't get to me, that seemed like a very exciting next step. (I mean, when was the last time I could go braless?) I left the office feeling on top of the world.

Showering

I was really nervous about taking a real shower, but I also couldn't wait. I turned on the warm water (not too hot!) and stepped into the shower with my back turned toward the shower head. Then, in a moment of bravery, I turned toward the water and allowed the water to spray directly on my upper chest. I used Dial anti-bacterial bar soap to carefully wash myself. It felt so good when all the smeared dried blood washed off. It was painful to lift my arms, so I leaned my head downward to wash my hair.

I could immediately see what Dr. Johnson meant about desensitizing myself. Before the shower, I felt so sensitive that I didn't even want air touching me, and I flinched anytime my dogs or my husband got near me. I was so afraid I would be touched. But when the warm water cascaded down my body and I washed myself, I was teaching my brain to be less reactive. It was a nifty psychological trick.

When I finished my shower, I towel dried off being careful to blot the water from my breasts instead of rubbing. I applied scar tape. Because I was still weak and sore, the shower took all my energy.

Q: What about bras? Are you still wearing the compression bra?

Okay, now this is where things get fun. First of all, I didn't mention buying bras until now for a reason. Before the surgery, you cannot be sure of exactly what size you will be.

Dr. Johnson recommended I continue to wear the compression bra at night. During the day, he advised that I could wear other front closure bras. No underwires allowed! He advised that I find something with support on the sides, or that I use lipo foam.

Q: What is lipo foam?

Lipo foam is another item you can buy on Amazon. It's a 1-2 inch thick firm foam that comes in sheets about the size of standard paper. You can use scissors and cut out a piece of foam that fits into the sides of your bra. This will provide extra pressure and support to the sides of your breasts, helping them heal in a forward-facing position.

So now we can talk about bras!

At this point, I could estimate my size close enough to get a few new bras. I spoke to many other women about this, and I bought several bras just to test them. The ones that worked well for me are the following:

- Fruit of the Loom front closure bras that come in a three pack. I got them from Amazon. There are pads included which can be removed from the bra, but I liked the pads. They camouflaged my nipples, which suddenly stood out more after surgery. I couldn't believe I actually wanted the padding. This was so different than what I was accustomed to when I was carrying around my big, droopy melons.
- I bought some front closing sports bras from thrift stores such as Goodwill, Savers, The Salvation Army, or the little thrift shop near me called Toni's. That way, if I estimated my size incorrectly, I

wasn't blowing a lot of money. It turned out I was a standard XL in sports bras and a very tight C-cup.

Q: What if the bras irritate my incisions?

I learned a very clever fix for that from speaking to Rosa: Buy some mitten clips! You can clip the bottom of your bra on one end and clip the other end on your pants. It keeps your bra from slipping upward onto your incisions.

Another tip I learned from Jill is to wear a tank top under your bra to avoid the bra rubbing.

15

WEEKS 3-6

Healing is the return of the memory of wholeness.
-Deepak Chopra

At this point, your main focus should still be to take care of yourself. You must rest, realize your limitations, and put yourself first. Don't take on laundry or dishes or vacuuming, even if you feel energetic enough to do it. You could possibly do more damage than good.

For the next several weeks, this was my life:
- Get out of bed and take a shower.
- Put on scar tape and a bra with the lipo foam. Get dressed.
- Bring my basket with my supplies to the recliner couch.
- Put on my mastectomy pillow (so comforting!).
- Rest. Watch tv. Text my friends. Go on social media. I did whatever I could do to keep my mind busy while my body stayed still.
- Walk around occasionally. Every couple of hours, I would get up

and walk around for circulation.
- Prepare my easy-to-make meals and eat regularly.
- Drink plenty of water.
- Apply ice and heat.
- Perform lymph node draining techniques.
- Rest, rest and more rest.
- Go to bed, sleeping upright on the wedge pillow.

I did actually get out and see friends occasionally, but I couldn't hug anyone or be vigorously enthusiastic about anything. That would have been too painful. But for the most part, healing is boring. I was hyper-focused on my pain and I complained a lot. I again used guided meditation to help me with the mental aspect of the pain.

I lamented that my healing was taking too long, and as the six week mark was looming ahead, I was worried I wouldn't feel well enough to work when I was scheduled to. But by some miracle, exactly at the six week mark, I felt just well enough to be ready to return to my job and my regular life.

16

THE MAGIC LINE

Healing is a matter of time, but it is sometimes also a matter of opportunity.
-Hippocrates

Right at the six week mark, I turned a corner and started to feel much better. It was like I crossed a magic line! I was able to start sleeping on my side (thank goodness!) as long as I was careful. I still felt very tender, so I used a couple of pillows to hold onto and keep my arms from squeezing together and thus squeezing my breasts together.

I was suddenly able to get back to work. I was able to take care of my house. I was able to do so many more things!

Q: Do I still need to keep using the scar tape?

Dr. Johnson recommended that at this point, I can simply use lotion to moisturize my incisions. Many women have expressed their preferences

on which lotions they used, and this is a basic list:
- Vaseline
- Cocoa Butter (I found this too thick, but many women swear by it.)
- Coconut oil
- Aquafor lotion
- Vitamin E
- Other body lotion

Your doctor may recommend that when you put the lotion onto your scars, that you engage in gentle scar massage in this way: Apply enough pressure with your fingers that the scar area appears white. Massage in circular motions, up and down motions, and side to side motions. You can also perform these massages while showering using your favorite soap.

Q: What was it like going back to work?

At exactly the six week mark, I definitely felt a huge improvement in my pain and energy but I still had achey breasts, sensitive nipples, and a slight lack of energy. However, when I pulled up my chair and started focusing on my work, it was actually a nice distraction. It felt good to be getting back into the swing of things. I had missed living my normal life, and it was exciting to get back to it.

Six weeks sounds like a long time, but it passed by so quickly. And now that I was feeling better, the really fun stuff started to happen.

Q: Once the surgery is complete and some of the swelling has gone down, can I get new bras now?

THE MAGIC LINE

YES! This is such an exciting time. But remember, your breasts will still be a bit swollen and the sides may still be swollen if you chose to have the side liposuction. However, I found that I couldn't wait much longer to buy bras! You've probably been looking at yourself in the mirror constantly, getting used to seeing your new figure. You've probably fantasized about wearing pretty new bras. I couldn't wait to get rid of the old ones!

Q: How did you know your size?

Since my breasts were so high and tight, I worried that I was too small. I thought maybe I was a B-cup, so I ordered a couple of bras in that size and found them to be too small. I should have measured.

Q: How do you discover your correct size?

Use the bra measuring method. I referred to an article in Good Housekeeping written by Jessica Teich. She provided great information including a chart.

- Step 1: Find your bra band size – Put on an unlined, non-padded bra or a fitted tee shirt. Run the measuring tape all the way around your back where the band sits. Keep the tape level. "Take a couple of deep breaths and make sure the band isn't too snug – you should be able to comfortably fit two fingers beneath the tape measure," says Emma Seymour, senior product analysis in the Good Housekeeping Institute Textiles lab.

If you don't get a whole number or you get an odd bra size number like 33, round up to the nearest whole even number. That number is your band size.

- Step 2: Measure your bust – run the measuring tape around your back and around the fullest part of your breast. The tape should just skim your breasts.
- Step 3 – Calculate your cup size – Subtract your band size from your bust measurement and find the difference. For example, my band measurement was 38 and my bust measurement was 41. The difference was 3. Here's the chart to determine the cup size.

<1 = AA
1 = A
2 = B
3 = C
4 = D
5 = DD/E
6 = DDD/F
7 = DDDD/G
8 = H

Q: So you ended up a 38C. Does that mean you can order and buy any bra in that size?

No! I was so excited about my new figure that I went crazy and bought a ton of adorable bras. I learned which ones worked for me. The bras that fit me best were the ones that had some stretch, and did not have molded cups. Although I measured a C, my breasts did not fill out a molded cup.

According to Jessica Teich, just because you found your correct bra size doesn't mean every bra will be correct for your breast shape. This is her advice:

- Round breasts carry fullness all over, and experts recommend triangle or plunge bras that hug breasts without digging in.
- Teardrop breasts carry most of the fullness on the bottom. Try sweetheart demi silhouettes or fabric overlays that keep cups laying flat.
- Compact breasts sit high, and you might find that lace or fabric doesn't lie flat and the bra sits away from the body. She advises shop for stretch fabrics or bras with padding.
- Wide-set breasts carry fullness on the sides. Look for bras with a generous space center part between the breasts (called the gores), and gently curving underwires.

Jessica goes on to advise on how to know if the bra fits correctly:

- The band sits level around your ribcage without riding up or squeezing.
- The center of the bra lays completely flat against the breast bone.
- The straps fit snugly without digging in. They should be adjusted to fit tightly for support, but without digging in.
- The cups don't gape or dig into the breasts even when moving. Be sure to wiggle around a bit in the bra to see how your breasts settle into the cups. Check the sides and front for spillage.
- Raise your arms. If the bra stays in place, you found a good one.

Q: Will my breasts always be high and tight?

No. You will hear the expression "drop and fluff" when talking about post-breast reduction results. This means that at some point, your breasts will relax, move a bit lower, and fluff out a bit instead of being held tightly against the body. Drop and fluff.

Q: What about sports bras?

Sports bras don't usually have molded cups. In fact, most of them come in sizes that do not include the cup size such as small, medium, large and extra-large. (I buy extra-large sports bras because of my band size 38.) At six weeks, I could raise my arms so I could buy sports bras and clothes that I put on over my head.

Q: Do you really need a sports bra?

Dr. Johnson advised that I wear a sports bra anytime during exercise such as walking or running. Sports bras also feel really comfortable now that I'm smaller. They feel like I'm wearing a giant hug. They do hold my breasts very firmly to my body, so I almost feel flat chested when I wear one. I have come to really enjoy that feeling. I can run, jump, do aerobics, and when I am doing yoga, my breasts no longer get in the way or fall out of my bra. It's wonderful!

Q: I can't wait to get rid of my huge, ugly bras! Is it time to dump them?

I'm right there with you. Right after my surgery, I knew I would no longer ever need those bras again, so I got rid of all but one. I kept my favorite big bra so that I could occasionally get it out, put it on, and clearly see the changes in my figure. It's like losing 100 pounds but keeping one pair of pants for comparison.

Q: Why did you need padding?

Not all of my bras have padding. The only reason I put some of the padding into my bras is to hide my pointy nipples.

Q: Can you go braless?

YES, YES, YES!! have not gone braless since I hit puberty, but then I realized "now is my chance!" However, as I mentioned, my nipples are very prominent (because they're actually facing forward), so I searched and found an amazing product to hide them. They are called nipple covers or "cakes" and can be worn under your clothing instead of a bra. They are flesh colored silicone circles that you put on your nipples. No adhesive needed as they cling to your warm skin. They cost around $16-$20 for a set, can be worn for many hours, and are reusable up to 30 times.

This is what I bought from Amazon and worked perfectly: GreatStyler classic nipple pasties in color nude. I could have bought any brand as long as I didn't have to use adhesive. This brand had great reviews.

Some brands have various colors to match your skin tone, so if your skin is a darker tone, this is what I found on Amazon: Prettywell nipple covers for women.They come in nude, caramel and cocoa.

Q: Speaking of nipples, did they look different after surgery?

Oh yes, in a great way! Over the years, as my breasts stretched and grew, the areola of my nipples got bigger and bigger. They looked like little salami slices on my breasts.

When Dr. Johnson trimmed around my nipples, he trimmed off the extra areola.(He even trimmed off the skin where I had this annoying black hair that I had to constantly pluck!) These days, when I look at my breasts, I can't help thinking that my nipples look adorable!

Q: After surgery, did you look thinner?

Yes! The extra weight had been removed from my chest, and I looked more balanced and much thinner. I sent pictures of myself dressed in fitted clothing to family members and friends, and they all told me I looked amazing.

Q: What if I have a big belly or big hips? Will I look unbalanced?

I also have a belly and big hips. However, I find myself standing upright which slims out my whole figure. Now that the melons are manageable, my shoulders and neck feel free, and I can stand proudly with my chest out. I feel so much more confident now that my breasts are a manageable size.

I also discovered that after my surgery, I became really motivated to take better care of my body. I resumed my diet and exercise routine and felt determined to look and feel my best. A lot of women have reported heightened motivation after surgery.

Q: What if I notice "dog ears"?

"Dog ears" is the term used to describe the puckering that can occur at the end of each incision. In my case, I had one dog ear on my left side but it went away after a period of time. If dog ears persist, most surgeons will correct the dog ears with a simple in-office procedure using local anesthesia.

Q: Was it exciting buying new clothes?

Oh my gosh, yes! The first chance I got, I went shopping. I frequent thrift stores, so it wasn't as expensive to experiment with different tops. I discovered I no longer gravitated to clothing that was loose and would hide my figure. I fit into clothing one size smaller than I was used to buying, not having to accommodate a tremendous weight on my chest. I bought strapless, halters, racer backs, and spaghetti straps… tops I only dreamed of before.

Another thing I wanted was a classic white, button-down shirt. In my previous life, button down shirts did not work. My breasts would always put pressure on the buttons which would create gaps. But not anymore! I was able to make this dream come true.

I can't tell you how exciting it still is to buy clothes. Every time I go to the thrift shop, I buy another load of new tops. Nowadays, it's like an obsession.

Q: Speaking of obsession, when will I stop being obsessed with my breasts?

It takes time. After my surgery, I find myself obsessed with looking at people's breasts on television and comparing them to my own. And every time I take a shower or get dressed, I can't help looking at myself in the mirror.It is taking time to wrap my mind around my new size.

Posture

Q: How do you get used to standing upright?

It actually takes practice. I went to my chiropractor after a few months of healing to discuss my lingering back pain. I explained to him that I'm still slouching even though I don't feel the weight on my chest that I used to feel. He suggested several stretches and some strength exercises to build up my back muscles and loosen my chest.

He said that because of the breast reduction and healing process, my body was sort of tightening up in the front. Intuitively, this made a lot of sense to me. (After approximately eight weeks of healing, I was cleared by Dr. Johnson to carefully stretch my upper body.) My chiropractor suggested a routine that I still follow. If I feel any pain in my breasts doing these, I stop.

I use a stretchy resistance band to strengthen my upper back muscles. I hold the band in both hands in front of my body, my arms at a 90 degree angle. Keeping my elbows at my sides, I then pull my hands apart putting resistance on my upper back and shoulder muscles. I then return them to center. This has reduced a lot of the pain I experienced in my back for years having oversized breasts.

I do floor stretches to loosen my chest muscles. I put down a yoga mat or small blanket on the floor and lie down on my back. I put my arms in a series of different positions to stretch my chest.

1. I put my arms straight out to my sides like a big T and rest for 10-20 seconds.
2. I bend my elbows 90 degrees and lay my arms completely on the ground. This pulls a little bit more on my chest muscles and feels really good. I rest there for 10-20 seconds.
3. I raise my arms above my head like I'm signaling "Touchdown" and lay them on the floor. This is a more advanced stretch, so I am

extremely careful. Once able to comfortably hold that position, I hold it for 10-20 seconds.
4. I do body twists. Laying on the yoga mat, I lay on my side. I bend the top leg and move it to the other side of my body in a twisting motion. I then move my top shoulder in the opposite direction, twisting my body even further. I take deep breaths and relax my muscles, despite the effort. I hold the position for approximately 20 seconds, and then do it again on the other side.
5. I have begun to add this stretch to my regimen. I stand in a door frame and put my hands on the frame at about waist level. I walk slightly through the door, feeling the stretch in my mid-section and lower chest. I then raise my hands on the door frame a little higher, and then walk a step forward in the door. I then keep raising my arms slightly higher on the door frame and pushing forward to stretch.

While performing any stretching techniques, it's essential that you remain aware of your body's reaction. **If you feel any pain, ease up.**

17

ACCEPTANCE

Once you accept that fact that you're not perfect, then you can develop some confidence.
-Rosalynn Carter

If only you could sense how important you are to the lives of those you meet; how important you can be to people you may never even dream of. There is something of yourself that you leave at every meeting with another person.
-Fred Rogers

This is the time to refocus ourselves to the whole person that we each are. You are not your breasts. Your figure is just part of you… you are so much more. This is the time to practice self-acceptance.

You may find that when the swelling goes down, you're smaller or larger than you envisioned. We can't predict the exact results; we can only plan our best. You are probably pretty happy with your results, despite any slight imperfections, and are feeling a great improvement in your back and neck pain.

After the surgery is complete and the hardest part of the healing process has passed, this is when it's very important to practice self-acceptance. It can help you feel better about yourself and more capable of dealing with life's challenges, leading to a sense of belonging. Some characteristics of self-acceptance include:
- Seeing yourself accurately
- Embracing all parts of yourself, positive and negative
- Accepting your values, preferences, feelings, and actions
- Recognizing your strengths and accomplishments
- Having a positive attitude toward yourself

This is the time to cultivate loving compassion for yourself, and to accept your body even with any perceived flaws. It helped me to listen to some guided meditations on self-acceptance. The one I enjoyed was called "Sleep & Magnify Self Love, Self Respect, and Self Acceptance" on YouTube by Pura Rasa – Guided Meditations. I highly recommend it.

18

BODY DYSMORPHIA

If he only wants you for your breasts, legs, and thighs,
Send him to KFC.
-Drake

A few women I've talked to have stated that some level of body dysmorphia arose in their lives after the surgery.

Q: What is Body Dysmorphia?

Body Dysmorphia is a disorder in which the sufferer is constantly obsessed with what she believes is a flaw in her appearance. A lot of people with this disorder also have eating disorders, but it can apply to anyone that is overly obsessed with her flaws.

The Body Dysphorphia Disorder Foundation has a free test you can take to determine if you are going through this. Just go to bddfoundation.org.

According to Johns Hopkins University, some of the symptoms of Body Dysmorphia are as follows:
- Trying to hide your body part under clothing or a scarf
- Constantly exercising or grooming
- Constantly comparing yourself with others
- Always asking people if you look OK
- Not believing others when they tell you that you look good
- Constantly checking yourself in the mirror
- Avoiding social activities because of how you look
- Not wanting to leave the house during the day.
- Feeling anxious, depressed, or ashamed of your looks
- Seeing many healthcare providers about your appearance
- Thinking of suicide

For a few months after surgery, it's very normal to constantly observe your appearance and to have a critical eye. We all do this. But with time, your inner critic should be slowly silenced as you begin to accept the new you.

If you find that your obsession with your looks is interfering with your daily activities, please do one of the following:

- Call your mental health provider. If you are already in counseling, please contact the provider who sees you and knows you. They may have various treatment options.
- Speak to your primary care physician.
- Reach out to a friend or relative.
- Contact your minister or spiritual leader.

19

ACTUAL HARM

Q: What if I have a legitimate reason to be unhappy with my results?

In some cases, you may have encountered serious complications that could have been avoided. If you are significantly unhappy with your results, your plastic surgeon may offer to do corrective surgery at no charge. Revision can be considered as early as 6-12 months after your initial surgery. Keep in mind that your original surgeon may not be willing to provide further care if you've already filed a medical board complaint or posted a negative review.

Some of the women I've spoken with are considering revisions.

Binky says:
Everyone told me it was the swelling. It wasn't. I'm 7 months post op and look just as big. I asked to be a 30dd not a 30ff!

Q: How can I tell the surgeon I'm unhappy with my results:
1. Reflect on your concerns and get clear on exactly why you are unhappy.
2. Schedule a follow-up appointment.
3. Prepare for the conversation. It would help to write down some notes on what you'd like to say.
4. Express your concerns calmly with the surgeon. Speak about facts and not feelings.
5. Listen to your surgeon's perspective. They may have a legitimate reason for the way your surgery proceeded.
6. Discuss possible solutions. Your surgeon may offer to do a revision.
7. Seek a second opinion if necessary. If, after completing these steps, you believe your original surgeon does not understand what want, does not validate your concerns, or is resistant to finding a solution, then you may need to see another surgeon.

Q: Do I have any recourse?

Complications can happen even with the very best surgeons. But if you feel you've truly been harmed by your surgery, I recommend that you document all the conversations you've had with your surgeon. Include written notes, dates, times, symptoms, problems, and any photos.

When you have all your documentation, you can file a complaint with the state medical board and/or with the office of Professional Medical Conduct. You may even decide to contact an attorney who specializes in medical malpractice on the grounds that the procedure exceeded the surgeon's qualifications. Many of these types of attorneys take your case with no upfront costs and only require payment when you win your case.

Most states have a statute of limitations to file a medical malpractice claim. In Arizona where I live, the Arizona Revised Statutes section 12-542 states that you can file a malpractice case within two years of the event. Check with your own state if you feel you have been injured.

20

THE RESULTS

After approximately six months, the swelling and bruising was gone. My breasts did soften a bit and I was functioning at 100% in my daily life. I became incredibly grateful that I had gone forward with my breast reduction. My shoulders and back are no longer in constant pain. I can sit up straight. I can walk, run, and jump with barely any jiggling. My husband loves riding on rough mountain roads in our Jeep, and now that my breasts aren't constantly bouncing on my lap and into my face, I enjoy it, too.

As I mentioned at the beginning of the book, breast reduction patients are statistically the happiest plastic surgery patients. The results are not just aesthetic, but also functional. It can be life changing!

Mackenzie stated:

7 days post op today and feeling amazing! This has seriously been the easiest recovery...Never took the pain meds and haven't taken Tylenol since the day after surgery...went from 36E to 34C with reduction, lift, and side lipo. This has seriously been the BEST decision of my life!

Yasmine says:
I went from an O to a C despite my surgeon telling me to go to DD. I've never been happier with my decision.

I spoke to Aimee and she is thrilled:
I am only seven weeks post op, but my surgeon took me down nine cup sizes, so I am very, very happy!! It will be a while before things settle and scars fade...but yes, very happy.

Nancy experienced immediate relief in her back pain:
After a 7 pound removal that was causing back issues, I am now a size 48a...And yes, I'd do it all over again. My back issues are gone and no more chiropractor bills!

And Beth said
I'm 2 years post op. Perfect proportion to my petite frame.

After a few months, I was elated with the results. I could still feel the incisions, like a constant awareness, but the pain was gone. I am now experiencing my life in this new figure, and it is glorious! It was worth all the money, time, and pain. It was so worth it all.

THE RESULTS

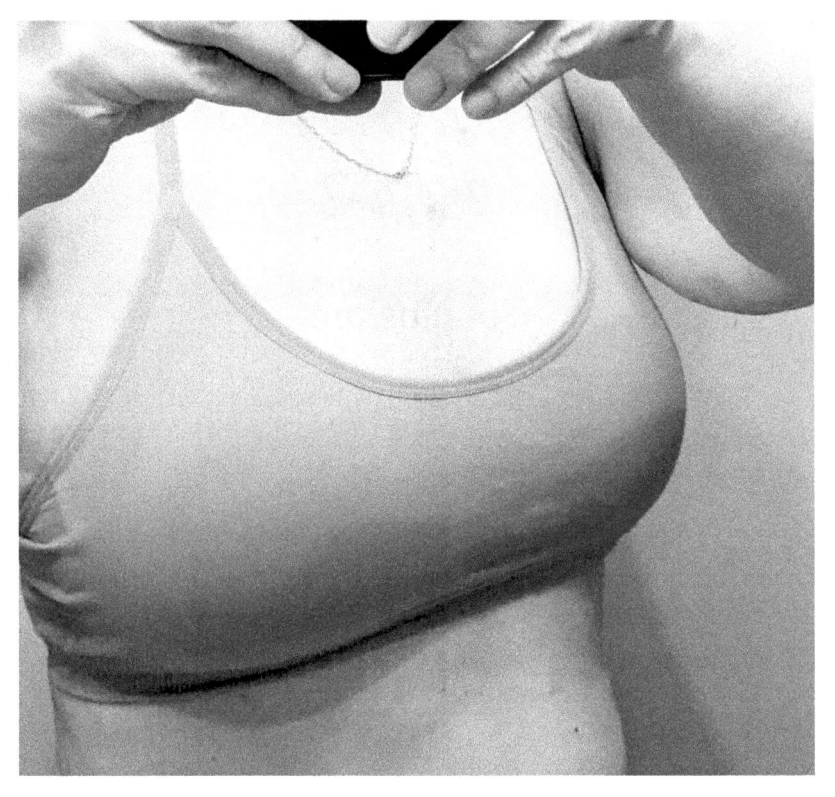

a light bra with padding

21

Conclusion

EMBRACING YOUR TRANSFORMATION

It's only after you've stepped outside your comfort zone that you begin to change, grow, and transform. -Roy T. Bennett

As you close this chapter and step into the next phase of your journey, remember that preparing for surgery, healing emotionally and physically, and embracing your new figure are all deeply interconnected. Surgery is not just a medical procedure; it's a transformative experience that requires care, patience, and resilience.

Approaching surgery with a prepared body and mind is key to ensuring a smooth experience. Educate yourself about the procedure, set realistic expectations, and assemble a supportive team of medical professionals, loved ones, and friends. Focus on nourishing your body with healthy food, and foster a calm, positive mindset. These steps will not only enhance your physical readiness but also lay a foundation for emotional

CONCLUSION

strength.

Recovery is a journey, not a race. Be kind to yourself as you heal physically, allowing your body the time it needs to adapt and rebuild. Equally important is addressing your emotional well-being. It's natural to experience a mix of feelings after surgery – joy, uncertainty, or even vulnerability. Acknowledge your feelings, and celebrate each milestone, no matter how small.

As you step into a new chapter with your transformed figure, embrace the opportunity to redefine how you see and celebrate yourself. This is a time to build confidence, strengthen relationships, and pursue the activities that bring you joy.

You will be taking a brave step to prioritize your health and happiness. By preparing for surgery thoughtfully, healing with patience, and embracing your new self with gratitude, you've unlocked the potential to lead a life filled with confidence, resilience, and fulfillment. Your transformation is a testament to your strength- both inside and out. Now, step forward boldly and live the happy, empowered life you deserve.

About the Author

Kerry Ann Rouse is a writer and artist living near Phoenix, Arizona with her musician husband, Mike, and their two playful dogs. She enjoys exploring the Arizona landscape in their Jeep or camper, playing a little piano, and relaxing with her family. Her passion for sharing her experiences and connecting with others shines in her work, offering readers both insight and inspiration.

You can connect with me on:
- https://www.kerryannrouse.com
- https://www.instagram.com/kerryannrouse